MORNING REIGN

ANOINTED CHRISTIAN POETRY
FROM THE HEART OF GOD

JOHN MARINELLI

Morning Reign
Ocala, Florida John Marinelli
All rights reserved
First Edition 2022

Print ISBN # 978-1-0880-3336-4
eBook ISBN # 978-1-0880-3340-1

Cover design and Formatting…Streetlight Graphics

This book is protected under US copyright laws. Any reproduction or other use is prohibited without the written permission of the author and illustrator. No part of this book may be reproduced, scanned, or distributed in any printed or electronic form without written permission.

Free Audio Book download when you purchase this book. Use this link for more details: https://www.marinellichristianbooks.com/morning-reign-audio/

More books and Christian Ministry at: www.marinellichristianbooks.com

TABLE OF CONTENTS

Preface 1
Introduction 3
Gallery of Anointed Poems 11
    A Highway Called Holiness 13
    A Whisper In The Wind 14
    The Master Of The Sea 15
    The Angels Cry Holy 16
    Arm's Length 17
    Thy Soul To Keep 18
    Clutter 19
    Call Upon The Lord 20
    Ask Me Now 21
    For The Joy Set Before Him 22
    The "Way Maker" 24
    Fragile Flower Red 25
    From Tears To Smiles 26
    He Is Coming Again 27
    The Power of His Name 28
    Holy Spirit 29
    "I AM" There 30
    It Came To Pass 31
    Little Prisons 32

Title	Page
The Creation Groans	33
Our Time of Prayer	34
Passing Over	35
Signs of The Times	36
Rest My Child	37
See Oh Man	38
Beyond The Rainbow	39
Stinking Thinking	40
In The Twinkle of An Eye	41
A Rock Higher Than I	42
The Caveman's Prayer	43
The Lighthouse	44
God's Little Two By Four	45
The Lord Is	46
The Master's Love	47
The Steps of A Good Man	48
The Pastor & The Master	49
Prayer	50
Two Houses	51
There Is Still Time	52
With Eagles' Wings	53
With Earthen Vessels	54
The "I Don't Know" Scenario	55
The Wrath of God	56
Consider The Clock	57
Is That All There Is?	58
Portrait of the Dammed	59
With Open Arms	60

Agreeing With God	61
I Find Myself In God	62
Passing Over	63
Anger And Fools	64
Forgiveness	65
Storms	66
Tongues of Hell's Fire	67
Our Greatest Fan	68
The Lord Is Greater	69
Rejoice With Me	70
Shout The Victory	71
You're Going to be Just Fine	72
So Listen Up	73
Winning The Battle	74
Choose Your Words	75
I Surrender All	76
The Perfect Man	77
As A Man Thinks	78
Wise Men Still Seek Him	79
Conclusion	80
About The Author	81

PREFACE

I am an author and a poet. I have written and published over 16 books and am still going strong. Most all that I write is Christian in nature and very focused to a particular subject or concept that is Biblically alive. This book, Morning Reign is no different. It is actually Bible Truths in poetic verse. It is meant to reveal certain Christian concepts like Faith, Forgiveness, Love, etc.

I have taken the liberty to discuss the origins of Christian Poetry as well as types and differences between what is Christian and what is secular. There is also a comparison between what is inspired and what is anointed.

It is my hope that all who read my poetry will walk away with a renewed spirit and fresh sense of God's presence. Poems are selected at random so the reader can use the selection as a daily devotional.

INTRODUCTION

THE CHRISTIAN POETIC EXPRESSION

Inspirational poetry goes back to before the Old Testament prophets. In fact, according to Holman's Bible Dictionary, one third of the Old Testament is cast in poetry. Thirty-five Old Testament books contain poetic expressions that often include prophetic overtones.

From Genesis 2:23 through Zechariah 9-11:3, words of encouragement and religious instruction are evident. In some cases, as in most of the book of Isaiah, even future events are presented in poetry.

Prophecy and poetry have been teammates through the centuries. Their voices cry out to a lost and dying world. They speak to a troubled church. Both declare the majesty and glory of God.

It was the 1st century Christians, however, that led the way for modern Christian poetry. Their relationship with Jesus inspired their writings as they focused their attention on being in harmony with God. The result was an in-filling of love, joy, peace, compassion, and a host of other deep emotions that gave evidence of their love for God and their faith in Jesus Christ. Out of this inspiration came a poetic expression that we now call Christian.

This uniquely Christian expression was and still is characterized by three separate and distinct factors: **Co-Authorship, Christian Focus,** and **Spiritual Unity.** These are the building blocks of good Christian poetry.

Co-Authorship is the trademark of all Christian poetry. The inspiration comes from the same Holy Spirit that moved upon the prophets of old. However, this time, it's from an indwelling presence rather than an overshadowing anointing that fell only to depart again. The inspiration is from God and the style is from the poet. Together they form the content of the poetic expression

Christian Focus: The focus of all Christian poetry is on the Christian experience through a personal relationship with Jesus Christ. The poet's inspiration is more personal in nature than even traditional secular sources. Instead of the beauty of a tree, it is the glory of the one that created the tree that inspires the poet.

Spiritual Unity is a two-fold process that involves both redemption and restoration. Both are central to the overall message. Both validate the inspiration as truly being from God.

This unique partnership in poetry quickly spread into the main stream of the Christian experience. Suddenly and without warning, Jewish and Gentile Christians began to express their most intimate and personal experiences with God through poetry. Slowly but surely, a "Christian Poetic Expression" emerged outside of its Hebrew origins into the entire Christian world.

As the "Christian Poetic Expression" became evident in all ethnic groups, its pulse was felt in poems of praise, prayer, prophecy, and thanksgiving. Its voice was heard through poems that edified, declared, revealed, and encouraged.

Christian poetry quickly became therapeutic in nature. It calmed the troubled soul; it strengthened weary hearts and fostered faith. It offered comfort, blessings, guidance, encouragement, instruction, and even a gentle rebuke.

Many of today's Christian poets have their own Internet website and use computers as an everyday tool to compose, edit and log their work. They come from all nationalities, all denominations, all walks of life, all ethnic backgrounds, and all age groups. Their poetry is an expression of the times in which they live. They author poems on anti-abortion, human rights, as well as, love, praise, faith and the other relational aspects of their Christian walk.

Today's Christian poets share their gifting as a ministry of love. Their ministries include; comfort to the elderly, sending poetic letters of protest to local newspapers, penning poetic tracts for the lost and greeting cards for various holidays. Some even design giant poster poems for public display.

The "Christian Poetic Expression" is very alive and well in today's world. It has survived the trials and tribulations of over 2,000 years and will continue until Jesus returns. Its future lies in the hands of countless thousands of Christians who seek and enjoy Divine Inspiration. Its value is as good as the poet's relationship with Jesus. It's my pleasure to share my poetic expression with you.

INSPIRATION & ANOINTING

It is important to understand the difference between an Inspired poem and an anointed poem. The difference is what shapes secular poetry and sets Christian poetry apart in a class all by itself.

I know that many poets think their poetry is good and call it inspired. However, what is the source of their inspiration? I can remember looking at a big old oak tree as a little kid and thinking, what if I were a tree? Many years later I wrote a poem and titled it, "If I were A Tree." The inspiration for the poem was the memory of me, as a little kid looking at a big old tree. The tree inspired me to pen a poem to describe myself if I were a tree.

The poem became a song and ended up as a waltz and a country western version. The one thing it wasn't was anointed. Trees cannot anoint writers of poetry but God's Holy Spirit can. The fact that I penned a poem about a tree says only that I drew from my own things but when I write under the anointing of God, I write in partnership with God. He directs my thoughts and clarifies my feelings. He also gives me focus that keeps me from rambling.

Sometimes it is hard to distinguish between Inspiration and anointing. There is a fine line. One must look behind the poet into the source. If it is anointed, it will glorify God and his only begotten Son, Jesus. If it is anointed, it will have the ability to transcend the fleshy thoughts of this world and capture the reader's heart. The words are alive and they will minister to the soul of man.

See for yourself what I am trying to communicate. Here is my trees poem that is inspired by me childhood experiences.

IF I WERE A TREE

If I were a tree,
I'd fill the sky
For all to see
and wonder why.

I'd shade the world
on a hot summer day
And beckon to all
who passed my way.

I'd offer a branch
To a feathered friend
And grant a kiss
To the howling wind.

I'd sway
in a gentle evening breeze
and change the season
with falling leaves.

I'd be there for you
Come rain or shine.
Down thru the ages
Until the end of time.

And I'd stand tall
For all to see
That is
If I were a tree.

I think the poem is really good. It is focused and expresses how I would feel. It is, however, all about me. I am the subject of the poem and my feeling are the topic of discussion. There is nothing wrong with me as the subject. It just isn't anointed by the Spirit of God. He often lets us express ourselves without his intervention. Sometimes we do well and other times we do not.

A poem that is anointed usually ministers to the reader's soul. It will penetrate the depths of the heart and communicate directly with the person's spirit. It will have a message or a revelation or a truth of some kind that most often blessed and refreshes the reader.

Now let's look at an anointed poem to see the difference.

DON'T WORRY
(MATHEW 6:34)

Don't worry about tomorrow.
You did that yesterday.
Go on with your life,
And remember always to pray.

Ask and it shall be given to you,
But this great truth you already know.
REJOYCE AND BE HAPPY, Why?
Your harvest comes from what you sow.

I will say it again and even more,
Until it becomes crystal clear.
Tomorrow will take care of itself,
But worry is another word for fear.

Now here's what I want you to do.
Trust in the Lord and be of good cheer.
Drop the worry from your vocabulary
And cast out that demon of fear.

Why is this poem anointed? 1st of all, because it reveals the will of God, for man to be happy.2nd, It points the reader away from worry and fear that will destroy them. Finally, it directs the reader to go on with life, knowing that God knows his or her need and will provide.

This poem was given to me by the Holy Spirit for a particular person that was struggling under fear and drowning in worry. The poem was meant as a refreshing word that would nudge the weary soul on into a posture of faith.

We are called to believe the word of God. It is our lifeline, our manna in the morning and our hope of any sort of victory in life. Anointed poetry comes from the heart of God thru the poet to the intended recipient. The Holy Spirit and the poet operate as one to fashion the poem. That's what makes it anointed.

TYPES AND SHADOWS

As you read the selected poetry, you will see "Types & Shadows" Most Christian poetry fall into various types. Here is a list of some of those types: Comfort, Instructive, Revelation, Rebuke, Love and prophetic. There are more types. I'll let you discover them as you read.

I would say that Comfort is the biggest category because we often get confused, frustrated, lonely and afraid. Our Heavenly father is continually quieting our spirits and assuring us that everything will be alright.

The poem above, "Don't Worry" is a poem of comfort. It speaks to the fearful soul and calms the spirit. That's why we call it a Christian poem that is anointed by the Holy Spirit.

Some of the poems you will read contain shadows. You might even see Jesus in a shadow behind the words. In some cases, you might even feel his presence as you read or feel closer to God than ever before. That's another mark of a Christian poem.

GALLERY OF ANOINTED POEMS

From The Heart of God

A HIGHWAY CALLED HOLINESS

He placed my feet on
a highway called "Holiness"
that led my soul
to the throne of God.

Amidst the cheers of Angels,
I walk wearing His holy gown.
Onward towards heaven's throne,
while evil cast its awful frown.

My eyes were opened
that I might see
both the good and the evil
that sought after me.

I walk the highway called Holiness
that crosses all of time,
towards the throne of God,
leaving this world behind.

A WHISPER IN THE WIND

There's a whisper in the wind,
That lingers both day and night.
A champion of truth and justice,
By the power of His might.

A word in due season,
That echoes from deep within.
A voice out of nowhere,
Reproving the world of Sin.

Look there, in the street,
And here, by the shores of the sea.
There's a whisper hidden in the wind,
A voice from eternity.

There's a calling from God.
His voice is hidden in the wind.
In a whisper, He speaks to our hearts,
With the love and counsel of a friend.

Listen for the whisper,
All who seek to know.
It is God's Holy Spirit,
Telling you which way to go.

THE MASTER OF THE SEA

What manner of man is this,
That calms the wind and sea.
With only the wave of His hand,
He caused my fear to flee.

He calms the storms of life,
That rain down upon my soul.
He bore my sorrows and strife,
That I should be made whole.

He is the Master of the sea,
Over its waves that rise up to play.
His peace will calm my heart,
As I kneel to him and pray.

Who is this mighty man,
That rules the wind and sea?
His name is Jesus, the Christ,
Who took my place at Calvary.

JOHN MARINELLI

THE ANGELS CRY HOLY

The Angels cry "Holy,"
while sorrow fills the land.
For God's Judgment Day
is to come upon every man.

The Angels cry "Holy,"
while mankind goes astray,
rejecting the love of God,
to follow his own precarious way.

The Angels cry "Holy,"
knowing the terror of the Lord,
when all who dwell in sin
will suddenly be destroyed.

The Angels cry "Holy,"
waiting for all things new,
born of the Holy Spirit,
when God's Judgment is through.

The Angels cry "Holy,"
"Holy is the Lamb,"
waiting for the children of God
to join "The Great I AM"

ARM'S LENGTH

I hold the world at arm's length
That their choices may not interfere.
While they do their own thing,
I watch and wait over here.

My steps must not go their way
For it's not where I need to be.
The Lord has shown me the path
That will lead me to my destiny.

The call to follow them is strong
And pulls at me now and then.
But I know with-in my heart
That their way is full of sin.

I must move on in life
Beyond their beckoning call.
It's the right thing to do,
So I do not stumble or fall.

I will not be swayed
By family, friends or business deal.
Their secret thoughts are not mine
To consider, to admire or feel.

So I keep the world at arm's length
As I journey through this life.
My faith in Jesus will keep me strong
As I walk in His glorious light.

JOHN MARINELLI

THY SOUL TO KEEP

Open your eyes oh world of lust.
Hear the cries and woes of the just.
Oh harlot of this endless night,
prepare for your approaching plight.

And to the tyrants of this world,
who rape the earth and steal her pearl.
You who deny the living God,
shall be cut down by His mighty rod.

And to you who love His Holy name,
the just, the poor, the meek and the lame.
Be of good courage and cheer,
for the Lord of Host is very near.

To those who die alone,
and wander through life without a home,
and to the children who suffer and weep,
their souls shall the living God keep.

CLUTTER

Clutter keeps the mind confused,
As images dance through the night.
Lost among those unimportant thoughts,
Are the dreams that once shined bright.

An endless parade of fear and doubt,
Crowds the mind to destroy our day,
Ever soaring on the wings of the soul,
Until it has formed an evil array.

But clutter is by one's choice,
Of those who listen to its beat.
Better to face imaginations' due
Than to fall into utter defeat.

Be Quiet! Is our spirit's angry cry,
As we call upon the name of the Lord.
Silence is our heart's desired prayer,
Until our minds are again restored.

JOHN MARINELLI

CALL UPON THE LORD

When your burdens overwhelm you,
like a mighty raging sea.
Call upon the Lord, Jesus,
and He will set you free.

When your heartaches are many,
and life is difficult to understand.
Call upon the Lord, Jesus.
He will come and hold your hand.

When your friends reject you,
because you follow after Him,
Call upon the Lord, Jesus.
And keep yourself from sin.

When you fall into depression,
as though it were a giant pit.
Call upon the Lord, Jesus,
who will restore your joyful wit.

When you're saddened by the day
feeling lost and all alone.
Call upon the Lord, Jesus,
who will make His way known.

When you are weary and heavy laden,
tired from life's many tests.
Call upon the Lord, Jesus,
Who is sure to give you rest.

ASK ME NOW

Hello my child,
How are you today?
I waited for your call
And have much to say.

A word in due season,
To cause your faith to soar.
A morsel of truth,
To quiet the lion's roar.

So hear, my beloved,
Before you go on life's way,
For there's a special blessing
In what I have to say.

It's not by might nor by power,
That you should gain success.
But it's by my Holy Spirit
That you attain life's very best.

Ask me now, my child,
For all that you need,
For I bless everyone
That is willing to believe.

JOHN MARINELLI

FOR THE JOY SET BEFORE HIM

I could have lived forever,
As a simple mortal man.
I could have called 10,000 angels,
To help me to stand.

But I laid down my life
Despising the shame.
For the joy set before me,
Was your life to gain.

I could have stayed in heaven,
As the supreme ruler of all things.
I could have played among the stars,.
And listened for the flutter of angel's wings.

But I laid down my life,
Despising the shame.
For the joy set before me,
Was to know you by name.

I could have sent my armies,
To rid this world of sin.
I could have destroyed the Earth,
As I did way back then.

But I bore the suffering of the cross,
Despising the shame.
For the joy set before me,
Was to take away your pain.

I could have done a lot of things,
To make this world right.
Or I could have done nothing,
And ignored your plight.

But God so loved the world,
That I endured the shame.
For the joy set before me,
Was your love to gain.

JOHN MARINELLI

THE "WAY MAKER"

Only Jesus can make a way,
through the difficulties of life.
He alone is the Lord,
over life's sorrow and strife.

He is the "Way Maker,"
when there is no visible way.
He will make the way known,
as though it were the light of day.

He will make a way,
for those of humble heart.
He will clear away the rubble,
restoring what Satan broke apart.

Jesus is the "Way Maker."
a friend to all who are lost.
He has made the way,
paying sin's incredible cost.

The way to the Maker,
is through His only Son.
He alone is the "Way Maker,"
until life's battles are won.

FRAGILE FLOWER RED

As a flower in earthen sod,
I bloom for thee, oh God.
To blossom with the turn of spring,
to be to you, a beautiful thing.

I lift my Fragile Flower Red
upward from my earthen bed,
to draw light from God above,
strength and peace and joy and love.

As a flower, I bloom for Thee,
that passersby may stop and see.
Your fragrance and beauty I am,
flowered in grace as a man.

As a flower in earthen sod,
I bloom for Thee, oh God.
Upward, I lift my head,
as a Fragile Flower Red.

JOHN MARINELLI

FROM TEARS TO SMILES

They attack from every side.
Zing!! goes their arrows of pride.
Like demons up from the pit of hell,
They come to laugh at those who fell.

They care not how hard you've tried.
They're here to kill God's love inside.
But though insults come our way,
we'll still find peace most every day.

God is greater than all their dares.
The Holy Spirit proves He cares.
When we're faced with many trials,
God will replace our tears with smiles.

HE IS COMING AGAIN

(I THESSALONIANS CHAPTER 5)

The Lord is coming soon, they say.
But no one knows the hour or day.
It is said, He'll descend through a cloud,
with the shout of an Angel, clear and loud.

Jesus will come for the "Born Again,"
who are free from the power of sin.
Those who wait for that blessed day,
looking for Jesus to come their way.

He will return in the power of His might.
But for many, He is as a thief in the night.
While some watch and even pray,
others will continue to go astray.

But for those who do not sleep,
who lovingly sow and gently reap.
God has granted His peace of mind,
to keep them until the appointed time.

JOHN MARINELLI

THE POWER OF HIS NAME

The power of Jesus' Holy name,
has healed the sick and cured the lame.
It's opened the eyes of those once blind,
and sets men free, time after time.

The power of Jesus' matchless name,
was born thru suffering and shame.
When Jesus fought for the souls of men
and gained the victory over every sin.

The power of Jesus' glorious name,
is God's gift for all to claim.
Free for the asking and given in love,
to all who believe in God above.

Yes, there is power in Jesus' name.
That's the reason He came,
to free us from our every sin
and bring our hearts back to Him.

HOLY SPIRIT

Holy Spirit, Lord divine
Send your love and make it mine.
Come Lord Jesus, for all to see.
Holy Spirit, breathe on me.

Holy Spirit, Lord divine
Fill my heart with new wine.
Come Lord Jesus, hear my plea.
Holy Spirit, breathe on me.

Holy Spirit, Lord divine
Be my Lord, all the time.
Come Lord Jesus is my plea.
Holy Spirit, breathe on me.

Lord of glory, I come to Thee.
Holy Spirit, breathe on me.

JOHN MARINELLI

"I AM" THERE

"I AM" There,
At the end of your broken dreams,
Before the sun rises over your day,
Prior to those tear-filled streams.

"I AM" There,
Down that road of despair,
When all seems to be lost,
And no one seems to care.

"I AM" There,
Over all of life's twists and turns,
When tomorrow is all but gone,
And when you are full of concerns.

"I AM" There,
Sayeth the Lord of Host,
To bring you hope and peace,
And the power of my Holy Ghost.

"I AM" There,
To be sure you make it through,
In the midst of every trial,
To bless your life and deliver you.

"I AM" There

IT CAME TO PASS

Things often come to pass,
but seldom do they ever last.
They come into our busy day
for a while, and then pass away.

We hear their voices, loud and clear,
when they arrive and while they are here.
They speak both joy and misery,
some to you and some to me.

We say, "It came to pass,"
Or say, "It happened so fast."
Down life's beaten path
comes both love and wrath.

So say goodbye to sad and blue,
to all that is now troubling you.
For things will come, only to pass,
but God's love will always last.

JOHN MARINELLI

LITTLE PRISONS

Little prisons await
the lustful soul.
Bars of selfishness and pride
create dungeons of icy cold.

Prisons of shame and jealousy
fill the heart with utter despair.
Bars that separate from God
and those that really care.

Stand back! While the doors
are tightly closed,
sealing away your life,
to wither as a dying rose.

Beware of those little prisons
that trap the lustful soul.
Keep yourself free from sin,
thru faith in the Christ of old.

THE CREATION GROANS

The creatures' expectations
shall all come true.
Their earnest desire
is to see what God will do.

With groaning and longing,
from deep within,
the creatures wait,
for the deliverance of men.

Subjected to vanity
by the powers to be,
they too shall be delivered,
through the cross of Calvary.

With loving expectations,
all of creation groans inside,
waiting for the sons of God
so they can dwell by their side.

JOHN MARINELLI

OUR TIME OF PRAYER

Oh child of God,
Why do you despair?
My angels' camp
is around you everywhere.

You may not see
my guiding hand.
Yet I am with you,
and I understand.

You are troubled
about so many things.
Your eyes see nothing
of what my will brings.

Be of good courage,
and walk in the light.
Stand up for the truth,
in the power of my might.

For I love you dearly,
and will always be there.
Go now, my child
until our next time of prayer.

PASSING OVER
MARK 4:35-41

"Let us pass over unto the other side",
Said Jesus, at the Sea of Galilee.
His faith rested in His father's will,
And that He had a Divine destiny.

No wind or storm held the power,
To change His faith into fear.
He rested in His Father's word,
As His fearful disciples drew near.

But if we, Like Jesus,
Could keep our eyes on God's will,
No storm that comes our way,
Can say to our faith, "Be Still"

JOHN MARINELLI

SIGNS OF THE TIMES

Oh, that mankind would repent
And turn again unto the Lord,
For the time is fast approaching,
When all will be destroyed.

Sin is no longer called Sin
By the "Liberal Media" of our day.
Why even some of the church folks
Have fallen or been led astray.

Perversion is now known
As, "Being Gay."
Sex before marriage
Has the approval of our day.

The "Right Thing To Do"
Is now considered wrong,
By fools wheeling power,
Striving to be strong.

Oh, that we would repent
And give thanks unto the Lord,
For these are "Signs of The Times",
When all will be destroyed.

REST MY CHILD

Rest my child, says the Lord.
Take thy peace and be restored.
I have provided, thy mouth to feed.
From the beginning, I knew your need.

Do not worry, fret or even fear,
For, my child, I am always near
To bless thy soul with love and grace,
To be with thee, face to face.

Come, my child, near to my throne.
Do not allow your faith to roam.
For those who will not believe
Can never find rest in times of need.

My Word shall see you through.
My grace I freely give to you
That you should rest, thy soul to keep,
Forever delivered from unbelief.

JOHN MARINELLI

SEE OH MAN

See oh man, the trees.
They sway in heaven's breeze.
Some with ripened fruit,
Others barren to the root.

See oh man, the apple tree,
With the only fruit to see.
No oranges, figs or tangerine,
Only the apple, pure and clean.

See oh man; look with your heart,
At the fruit both sweet and tart.
Both life here & all eternity,
Await the fruit of your tree.

Time grows short till harvest comes.
When the fruits of life are all but done.
See oh man, what you will do.
For one day, God will ask fruit of you.

BEYOND THE RAINBOW

I traveled beyond the rainbow,
To see all that I could see.
I gazed at the beauty of the stars,
And looked into the door of eternity.

But when I stood up,
To see if there was more,
I saw the face of Love,
Smiling, as if to adore.

No words were ever spoken,
And yet I heard an awesome cry.
A voice that said, "I love you,"
As His shadow drew nigh.

Joy raced around my head,
And peace flowed within my soul.
I began to weep and laugh, and shout,
As His presence melted away the cold.

Finally I found forgiveness,
From all the sorrows of life.
The love of God set me free,
From my pain and inward strife.

Glory be to God and Jesus,
His only begotten Son.
He alone holds my future,
And declares that I have won.

STINKING THINKING

Stinking thinking, they say,
Is bad for your health.
For it frustrates life's goals,
And denies true happiness felt.

A right perspective is important,
As we think about everything.
It will either bring us down,
Or cause us to shout and sing.

What we think about these days,
Really does affect our life.
It can cause us to overflow with Joy,
Or fall into depression and strife.

So don't let your thinking,
Stink all the way up to heaven.
Stand in faith before God,
And get rid of that negative leaven.

IN THE TWINKLE OF AN EYE

In the twinkle of an eye,
The Lord will come for me.
Before you can even blink,
I'll be with Jesus in eternity.

In the twinkle of an eye,
The trump of God will sound,
And all who love the Lord
Will be homeward bound.

In the twinkle of an eye,
The World will fall into despair.
When God's wrath is poured out,
Upon all who do not care.

In the twinkle of an eye,
We shall shout the victory.
Spared from His judgment,
To complete our divine destiny.

In the twinkle of an eye,
Destined to come our way.
I long for that final blink,
When we all will shout, "Hurray"

JOHN MARINELLI

A ROCK HIGHER THAN I

Rock of Ages, draw me nigh
To a place that is higher than I.
Where peace and safety surely dwell
Far from the torment of an endless hell.

I stand in awe, Lord, of Thee,
Knowing that this is where I can be.
To hide in cover of gracious wing,
Makes my heart to laugh and sing.

My lips are full of wonderful praise.
My heart and hands I humbly raise
To Jesus, God's Ageless Rock.
I come, Lord, while others mock.

O Rock of Ages, draw me nigh
To a place that is higher than I
That I may dwell in perfect peace.
O Lord, what sweet release!

-|- Psalms 61 -|-

THE CAVEMAN'S PRAYER

Lord! I cannot see the light of day,
For this cave is dark and yet I pray.
Life has overwhelmed me on every side,
Because of oppression, fear and pride.

-|-

But you, oh Lord, are my strength,
My refuge in times of worry and fear.
You will deliver me from all of this,
And will gently draw my soul near.

-|-

I will yet stand victorious,
Even though I am in a cave.
Before I can see it happen,
I give you, Lord, all the praise.

-|-

For the light of day will come
And I will still give you praise,
For helping me through it all,
When I prayed in the cave.

-|- Psalm 142 -|-

JOHN MARINELLI

THE LIGHTHOUSE

A lighthouse is a blessing,
To the ships that toss in the sea,
For it shows them the way,
Until they can clearly see.

The rage of an angry storm
Cannot hide its brilliant light.
Nor can its awesome furry,
Rule as an endless night.

Jesus is the lighthouse,
For those who have gone astray.
The light of His love,
Offers a new and living way.

Jesus is the lighthouse,
When fear and sickness rage.
The light of His love,
Gives hope in difficult days.

So trust in the Lord,
And look for His light.
He alone is "The Lighthouse",
That guides you through the night.

GOD'S LITTLE TWO BY FOUR

God has a little 2' X 4'
That rest on heaven's windowsill.
He uses it now and then,
When we stray from His will.

Sometimes we need a good "Bap";
With the Lord's little 2' X 4'
To knock out the confusion,
And help us to desire Him more.

The Lord's little 2' X 4'
Is what we sometimes need,
To get our thinking straight,
And keep our focus indeed.

The Lord's little 2' X 4'
Is fashioned from life's every trial,
So we do not stray from His will,
Or fall into an ungodly lifestyle.

JOHN MARINELLI

THE LORD IS

The Lord is
The Savior of my soul.
By His stripes,
I am made whole.

The Lord Is
The Beginning & the End.
The Alpha & the Omega,
My very best friend.

The Lord Is
My refuge when things go wrong.
A shield & a Buckler,
From Satan's outstretched arm.

The Lord Is
God's perfect love, indeed
A very present help,
In times of need.

The Lord Is
Everything to me.
My hopes & dreams
My life & victory.

The Lord Is
Coming back some day,
As the King of kings
So watch & pray.

The Lord Is
The avenger of the just.
The Savior of this world,
In whom we put our trust.

THE MASTER'S LOVE

In the quiet of the hour,
I walk with my Lord each day.
Sometimes in prayerful thought
Of what the Master is about to say.

Oft times I sit in silence,
gazing into heaven's door,
wondering why it is,
that He chose me to adore.

My grace could never compare
with the beauty of a tree.
Why even the flowers
Are greater in stature than me.

Yet He watches over me
with tender loving care,
As a father loves his child,
My Lord is always there.

I listen for His voice,
As His presence draws near,
Knowing that the Master's love
Will wipe away every tear.

JOHN MARINELLI

THE STEPS OF A GOOD MAN

The steps of a good man
Are ordered by the Lord.
He leads us by still waters
Until our souls are restored.

Our pain and suffering
Are all taken away.
Replaced with great hope
For a brand-new day.

He orders our steps
By Holy Spirit's breath,
That we may overcome
Satan, Sin and Death.

The steps of a good man,
Are not entirely his own.
They're given by God
So he doesn't walk alone.

THE PASTOR & THE MASTER

If the pastor doesn't follow the Master,
Then I cannot follow the pastor.
But if the pastor walks with the Master,
Then I can walk with the pastor.

When pastors stray from the Master,
The sheep stray from the pastor.
But when the pastor loves the Master,
God blesses the sheep and the pastor.

Jesus is the pastor's Master,
And why the sheep follow the Master.
For He is Lord over the pastor.
That's why they call Him Master.

The pastor and the Master--
The Master and the pastor--
The sheep follow the pastor,
When the pastor follows the Master.

JOHN MARINELLI

PRAYER

Prayer is spoken words
uttered to God above,
either by voice aloud,
or through a mind of love.

Request for daily help
in life's every affair.
A plea for more power
to overcome Satan's snare.

A time to openly share
every concern of life.
Things that bring joy
and yes, even strife.

God hears every voice,
that calls to Him in prayer.
He knows their plight,
and every burden they bare.

So call upon the Lord
and never ever depart
and He will answer you,
In quietness of heart.

TWO HOUSES

We built our homes together,
Mine upon a Rock and his in the sand.
He thought his would be all right,
But he was a foolish man.

God's wisdom showed me the way.
And what I needed to do,
But my foolish neighbor,
Never had a clue.

Then the rains came,
And the winds began to blow.
The storms beat upon our homes,
And we had nowhere to go.

We built our homes together,
My neighbor and me.
Mine is still there upon the Rock,
But his ceased to be.

Wise men and fools both suffer,
The storms that befall mankind.
But those who trust in Jesus,
Will always stand the test of time.

JOHN MARINELLI

THERE IS STILL TIME

Inspired by God's love,
I pen this rhyme.
For you, dear friend,
while there is still time.

Hear my words,
for they are true.
Jesus, God's only Son,
gave His life for you.

A ransomed soul
on the cross of Calvary.
As a penalty for sin,
that you might go free.

Call upon Jesus,
to give you life anew.
His grace and power
will see you through.

God patiently awaits,
your humble cry.
Salvation is yours,
to accept or deny.

WITH EAGLES' WINGS

I mounted up with Eagles' Wings
to soar above the clouds.
I viewed life above its trials,
separate from the crowds.

Just me and God, together in the day,
His love to behold.
With Eagles' Wings, He led the way,
my future to unfold.

Forgiveness and peace in a distance,
suddenly I could see.
Joy and happiness trailed behind,
then overshadowed me.

With Eagles' Wings,
I soar above life's every trial.
Now I walk by word of faith,
rejoicing with every mile.

JOHN MARINELLI

WITH EARTHEN VESSELS

Earthen vessels have never shown
such glory that once was known.
Through time and all of eternity,
came the glory of His majesty.

Full of love and full of grace,
He dwelt among the human race
to heal the sick, the blind and the lame,
to free mankind from sin and shame.

With earthen vessel He conquered all
by perfect obedience to His destined call.
For this we praise His holy Name,
full of grace and full of fame.

The glory of His majesty
still shines through from eternity.
Again and again to meet life's call,
in earthen vessels to conquer all.

THE "I DON'T KNOW" SCENARIO

Here is the "I Don't Know" scenario.
I hope you will understand.
Because the future and everything else,
Is not really at our command.

Will it rain today?
I don't Know.
Will I live to be 100?
I don't know.

Will my bills get paid on time?
I don't know.
Life is full of "I Don't Knows",
Far too many for me.

There's a lot that "I Don't Know",
About this life and Eternity.
So I'll leave things up to God,
Who knows what will & will not be.

He will guide me by his Spirit,
Through life's Thick and Thin.
My times are in his hands.
He is my only true friend.

JOHN MARINELLI

THE WRATH OF GOD

The wrath of God shall surely come,
Upon those who choose not to see.
God will sit in the heavens,
And laugh at their calamity.

He will not protect the defiant,
Those who reject His love and majesty.
He turns them over to be reprobate,
Because they chose their own reality.

He will bring their mischief,
Upon their own foolish heads.
They will reap what they sow,
For that is what God said.

There is no escape from an angry God,
He will surely avenge His righteous name,
So stay close to the Lord in all you do
And His wrath will not fall on you.

CONSIDER THE CLOCK

Consider the clock
That ticks away the time,
Second by second as
You read this rhyme.

Listen at the passing
Of this beautiful day.
Observe how fast
Our lives pass away.

Today becomes tomorrow
When yesterday is done.
Dreams and aspirations
Become memories undone.

Both joy and sorrow
Pass through our day,
As though a child
Had come to play.

There's plenty of time
To do our own thing.
For in these moments
Life proudly sings.

But in the day
And this very hour,
Passes our lives
As a fragile flower.

Faster and faster
The time passes away,
As we boldly march
Through life's array.

Finally to stop
As does our times,
To listen as Judgment
Sounds its awful chimes.

JOHN MARINELLI

IS THAT ALL THERE IS?

Is that all there is?
Say everyone these days.
Because life has lost its luster,
Holding no joy of triumphant praise.

Is there no more to life
Than just getting by?
Is that all there is,
But to stop and reason why?

Come, let us ponder
Matters pursuant to the soul.
Things that make us happy,
And dreams that have grown old.

If that is all there is,
It could be a deceptive web.
A snare that's designed,
To cloud what God has said.

Or heaven's window,
Closed by disobedience.
And unwillingness to follow,
Good old common sense.

That's all there is,
Because no faith exists.
Only an acceptance,
Of that which persist.

But God is greater,
Than what now is.
He always responds,
To faith that lives.

-|- Hebrews 11-1 -|-

PORTRAIT OF THE DAMMED

They seek after peace of mind,
But make choices that
Do not rhyme.

They are giants made of sand
That fall apart when
It's time to stand.

They hear words of faith,
But turn a deaf ear until
It's just too late.

They seek after reason why,
But reject the truth
To believe a lie.

They believe that all is well,
But travel a road that
Leads to Hell.

JOHN MARINELLI

WITH OPEN ARMS

He waits, oh man, with open arms.
By Holy Spirit, He woos and charms.
Calling by name, thy sins to right,
Pleading, in love, for thee tonight.

Hear, oh man, His urgent request,
For time has few moments left.
Man, with all his deeds of crime,
Shall suddenly fall to God divine.

He waits, oh man, for you to say,
"Lord, forgive me, I'll now obey."
With open arms, He calls your name,
To join others who share His fame.

Come, oh man and find your way,
For God, through Jesus, holds the day.
Make Him Lord and you will find,
Love and Joy and Peace of Mind.

AGREEING WITH GOD

I'll speak of things that are not,
Believing in them as though they were,
Because my Heavenly Father spoke them first,
In glorious promises that never blur.

I'll take Him at His word,
And listen to all He has to say.
I'll wrap each promise around my soul,
Until what was spoken becomes my day.

I will agree with my Lord,
Trusting that He knows best,
For only His awesome power,
Can provide my soul with rest.

JOHN MARINELLI

I FIND MYSELF IN GOD

I find myself in God.
He is my, "Everything."
I know that He is Lord,
My I find life, my Hope, and King.

I find myself in God,
Not the ways of sin.
Nor do I look to others,
To know who I really am.

I find myself in God,
To whom I bow on bended knee.
He alone is my joy and strength
And where I want to be.

PASSING OVER

"Let us pass over unto the other side",
Said Jesus, at the Sea of Galilee.
His faith rested in His father's will,
And that He had a Divine destiny.

No wind or storm held the power,
To turn His faith into fear.
He rested in His Father's word,
As His fearful disciples drew near.

But if we, Like Jesus,
Could keep our eyes on God's will,
No storm that comes our way,
Can say to our faith, "Be Still"

ANGER AND FOOLS

Anger resides in the bosom of a fool
So the holy scriptures say
So it's ok to be angry
As long as it doesn't stay.

Things happen in life
That are sure to make us mad
Evil hides in shadows
To cause harm and make us sad

There are a thousand things
That can justify anger's rule
But we must not hold on to them
Lest we become the proverbial fool

So when anger grips your soul
Seeking to kill God's love inside
Do not let it hang around
Or give it a place to hide.

FORGIVENESS

Forgiveness offers freedom,
To the repentant soul.
It opens God's heart,
To forgive and make you whole.

God does not honor
The unrepentant heart.
Instead, He closes up heaven,
To keep Himself apart.

So forgive those
Who have offended you.
And God will be there,
To forgive and bless you.

JOHN MARINELLI

STORMS

Storms are common to this life
They howl with sorrow and strife
Like the rage of an angry sea
They flood the mind with imagery

Fear and worry soon enter our time
And confusion tags along to dine
Together they cast their evil web
Pain and sorrow until we're dead

But God is greater than the storms
He sets us free from all their scorn
Through submission to His will
The storms calm to a quiet still.

TONGUES OF HELL'S FIRE

The tongue is a little member of the body
It can speak truth that edifies to inspire.
Or be ablaze with angry words,
Straight from hell's tormenting fire.

Always destructive and full of hate,
Flaming with jealousy, pride and lust.
This is the tongue that knows not God,
And speaks from a lack of faith and trust.

Let not this tongue be yours to wag,
And be not like those that always do.
Both good and evil can flow off the tongue.
Allow only the good to come from you.

JOHN MARINELLI

OUR GREATEST FAN

God is faithful
Even when we are not.
He watches over His Word,
Crossing "T's" and dotting every dot.

He is a very present help
In times of sorrow and pain.
We can trust in His Word
For sunshine and latter rain.

He alone holds our future
In the palms of His hands.
He leads us as a loving Shepherd
Into green pastures and fruitful lands

God is faithful
To honor His covenant with man.
He, though LORD of all,
Is our greatest fan.

THE LORD IS GREATER

The Lord is clothed with majesty
And girded about with strength.
He is from old to everlasting,
Whose days are without length.

He is mightier than many waters
That rush over our emotional shore.
He is greater than their noise
And more powerful than their roar.

His house is adorned with Holiness,
And all His testimonies are true.
To God Be The Glory, Forever!
His awesome power will deliver you.

So look for the Lord in majestic beauty,
When the waves lift up their violent heads.
And listen for His calming quiet voice,
Among all the confusion, hear Him instead.

JOHN MARINELLI

REJOICE WITH ME

Oh child of God
Why do you cry for me?
It was my joy
To go to Calvary.

Through my pain,
You were healed.
In my suffering,
Your fate was sealed.

Oh child of God
Do not cry for me.
I came from heaven,
To set you free.

For you, my child
Death has no sting,
Because you made me
Your Lord and King.

Oh child of God
Rejoice with me,
For your name
Is written in eternity.

SHOUT THE VICTORY

Call upon the Lord.
He will not turn you away.
His wonderful grace,
Is meant for every day.

Reach out to Jesus,
In your time of need.
He is sure to deliver,
If you let Him lead.

Stand up in faith
In all that you do.
Speak not of things
That make you blue.

Be of good courage
In these last days.
Then lift up your hands,
In thanksgiving and praise.

Claim your salvation,
And shout the victory.
For Jesus has come,
To set you free.

JOHN MARINELLI

YOU'RE GOING TO BE JUST FINE

Our souls hath He restored.
He who? Of course, the Lord.
With His love and His peace divine,
He said, "You're Going to be Just Fine."

No more sorrow, sickness or pain,
Only His Joy, forever to reign.
As old things slowly pass away,
New things will appear each and every day.

Be of good courage and patiently wait.
God is never ever too late.
The Lord will see you through.
Why?, because He loves you.

Things will get better.
Wait and you will see.
God will hear your cry,
And come to set you free.

SO LISTEN UP

I write this verse that all should know.
What I have to say is like a seed ready to grow.
So listen up to all I have to say.
It could be the very blessing your heart needs today.

God has not given you a spirit of fear.
Instead, He has offered to dry up every tear.
He really loves you, even though you often fail.
His love and mercy follows you
Enabling you to be the head and not the tail.

So do not worry or even fret.
That's why Jesus paid Sin's awful debt.
Now go on in life to discover its victory
Knowing that Jesus has indeed set you free.

JOHN MARINELLI

WINNING THE BATTLE

We must use the Word of God
To calm emotions that fray.
For the enemy never sleeps
Until he has led us astray.

So when your emotions overflow
With feelings like depression and fear.
Know this! If you dwell in that place,
You invite the enemy to draw near.

When your emotions rage
With fiery darts aglow,
Stand in the power of the Lord
Against its awful woe.

And if you get confused
And lost in the storm,
Put your thoughts on trial
Rejecting all but heaven born.

You can win the battle
That rages within your soul.
By casting down imaginations
And breaking Satan's hold.

Remember to focus on Jesus
Holding the world at arm's length.
Lift up your head above the trial
And the Lord will give you strength.

CHOOSE YOUR WORDS

Choose your words with love and grace.
See a smile on every face.
Cross your words with evil eye,
and see the hearer break down and cry.

Wonderful words of life or evil words of heart…
They both pierce the soul, one sweet and the other tart.
So choose your words to make them say,
"Jesus loves you" or " Have a nice day"

JOHN MARINELLI

I SURRENDER ALL

I surrender all to Thee
My love, my life and liberty.
For if I should rule my throne,
You Lord, would stand-alone.

But with my will I offer Thee,
My love, my life and destiny.
That you should rule this throne.
So I'll never again stand alone.

I'd surrender all I have to Thee,
For but a glimpse of your majesty.
That I may live within your perfect love
Both here on earth and heaven above.

THE PERFECT MAN

The mature man of God
Walks in righteousness.
His life and testimony of earth
Is marked by a Godly rest.

The end of this type of man
Is the ability to walk in peace.
To see through life's annoyances
To find that sweet release.

Though attacked by Satan
Most every day and on every side,
The perfect man stays in his rest,
Knowing that Jesus will turn the tide

Faith and trust are real words
That do not fade away or easily depart.
For the perfect man is marked
With peace from God in his heart.

JOHN MARINELLI

AS A MAN THINKS

I am as my thoughts are
No matter what you say.
If I think good or bad thoughts,
That is what rules my day.

You cannot know me
As I really am,
Unless I reveal my thoughts
And become a transparent man

You are no different than me
Underneath all the fleshy show.
We all are as we continually think
Some happy and others full of woe.

So think on the things in life
That brings out the very best.
And you will surely get better
And be able to finally rest.

WISE MEN STILL SEEK HIM

Wise men still seek Him
Who appeared so long ago.
They come now by grace
Through faithful hearts aglow

Wise men still seek Him,
For He is their "Bread of Life"
A sustaining inner strength
Through times of sorrow or strife.

Wise men still seek Him
The Christ of Calvary
God's only begotten Son
Crucified as sin's penalty.

Wise men still seek Him,
Jesus, God in human array.
King of Kings and Lord of Lords,
Born to Earth on Christmas Day.

CONCLUSION

How do I conclude a poetry book when I have written over 500 poems? I guess I just have to stop. Well, I tried to select those poems that were more relevant to ministry and encouragement so my readers can be blessed. A poem a day would be the best way to read through so many poems. However, one more poem can't hurt. I will leave you with one final poem.

BE A BUTTERFLY

Be A Butterfly
And fly away with me.
We'll fly with God's Promises
Straight into eternity.

Be a butterfly
To crawl no more
But to soar in the Spirit
Above earth's mighty roar.

Be a butterfly
To fly to heights unknown,
Soaring on the wings of faith,
Never more to be alone.

Be a butterfly
And fly away with me,
For God has made us new.
At last! At Last! We are free.

ABOUT THE AUTHOR

JOHN MARINELLI

John Marinelli is an ordained minister; He has formed and been pastor of one church in Wisconsin and was the pastor of another in Alabama. He has also been a youth minister and evangelism director over the years.

John has authored several other books including: "Original Story Poems", "The Art of Writing Christian Poetry," "Pulpit Poems," "Moonlight & Mistletoe," "The Mysterious Stranger," "With Eagles Wings," "Mysteries & Miracles," "It Came To Pass," Why Do The Righteous Suffer," "Believer's Handbook of Battle Strategies," "An Elephant Named Clyde," and "The End of "The World From The Beginning,"

John is an accomplished Christian poet. He also dabbles in songwriting and writing one act Christian plays.

John now lives in north central Florida where he enjoys a retired lifestyle of singing karaoke, playing computer chess and writing Christian books.

More about the author can be obtained by visiting his website at www.marinellichristianbooks.com

www.ingramcontent.com/pod-product-compliance
Lightning Source LLC
Chambersburg PA
CBHW020430010526
44118CB00010B/503